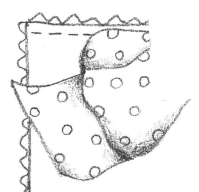

Funeral Potatoes
and Other
Potato Recipes to
Die for

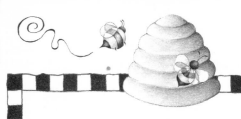

This book is one in a series of books called
"Bringing Back the
Old-Fashioned Art of Homemaking"

Published by Peggy Layton
P.O. Box 44
Manti, Utah
84642

Phone orders 435-835-0311
Cell Phone 435-851-0777
Online orders www.PeggyLayton.net

Wholesale pricing and discounts
are available for quantity sales,
Church, and Civic Groups.

ISBN: 1-893519-06-6
Published July 2005

A special thanks to all who helped

This book is dedicated to the many people who have given their love and support. The first one is my husband Scott Layton who learned to work on his dads onion farm in West Layton, Utah. I will always be grateful to him for instilling a love of the land in me and for the awesome potatoes he grows each year in our garden. It is a spiritual experience to grow a garden and there is magic in the soil.

To all my friends and relatives in Idaho who own potato farms in the Burley-Rupert area where I grew up. This is one of the reasons I wanted to write a cookbook about potatoes.

To my wonderful artists, Renae Lindgren www.renaelindgren.com and my best friend Linda Mickelson for the cover and inside art. They are "awesome".

To Debbie Harman for her creative ideas and helpful suggestions on the artwork and David Michael Noorlander for putting all the artwork onto a disk for printing.

To My cousin Marlin Mosher for his computer skills and for getting the cover art ready to print.

To my committee of taste testers for testing the recipes, rating them, and giving me helpful suggestions. Thanks to Lannette, Debbie, Kay, Leslie, Nola, Jan, Pauline, Cynthia, Suzann, Karen, Jennie, Carol, Kelly, Valerie, and Jessie.
The recipes that were rated (fabulous) by the taste testers are listed below the recipe.

To the scrapbook company called "Keeping Memories Alive, Inc." www.scrapbooks.com for permission to use their scrapbook paper for the cover of this book.

About the Author

Peggy Layton, A home economist holds a Bachelor of Science degree in Home Economics Education with a minor in Food Science and Nutrition from Brigham Young University.

Peggy is the author of a series of cookbooks on the subject of food storage and being prepared for emergencies. The latest book, published by Random House Publishing in New York is called "Emergency Food Storage and Survival Handbook". Other titles that are self published include: "Cookin' With Powdered Milk", "Cookin' With Dried Eggs", "Cookin' With Beans And Rice", "Food Storage 101" Where Do I Begin?, and she is a co author of the book "Cookin' With Home Storage".

Peggy has lived in Manti, Utah for over 20 years. She is married to Scott Layton and together they have seven children, two dogs, two cats, and enjoy raising chickens and growing an awesome garden. They own a "Growing Dome" greenhouse and enjoy fresh vegetables year round. They believe in provident living and practice what they preach. They live on close to an acre piece of property, completely free of debt and grow food year round as well as canning, dehydrating, and putting up all the produce from the garden and fruit trees on the property.

Peggy is very interested in health and nutrition. She is a Licensed Massage Therapist and specializes in "Emotional Release Therapy".

Peggy has traveled and lectured to groups all over the country, she keeps busy running two businesses, a mail order cookbook business and a massage therapy business.

Contents

Funeral Potatoes And Other Potato Recipes To Die For

Recipes

Funeral Potatoes

Baked Potatoes

Breads

Desserts

Fried Potatoes

Main And Side Dishes

Mashed Potatoes

Salads

Soups, Chowders, And Stews

Sweet Potatoes

Types of Potatoes

The most popular varieties of potatoes are: Russet, Round White, Round Red, Long White, Fingerling, Yellow Flesh, Blue and Purple, New or (freshly dug small potatoes), Instant, Sweet Potatoes and Yams. The Russet potatoes are the best for mashed, baked, hash browns and french fries. They are fluffy and light when mashed. Red potatoes are the best for potato salad because they are a more firm potato and do not go mushy when overcooked. Yellow Flesh potatoes are best when used in the funeral or au-gratin potato dishes. Instant potatoes are best used for mashed potatoes and dishes such as mashed potato casseroles. Dried potatoes can be reconstituted and used in any recipe calling for fresh potatoes.

Hints For Using Potatoes

1). The nutritional value of potatoes is higher when they are cooked with their skins on. The vitamins are found just beneath the skin. Potatoes are a good source of vitamin c, protein, energy rich starch and fiber.

2). To improve the flavor of old potatoes, add a pinch of sugar to the boiling water while they are cooking.

3). To prevent potatoes from turning brown after you have peeled and exposed them to air, add a teaspoon of white vinegar to a bowl of water, soak the potatoes for about 20 minutes, drain the water and pat them dry with a paper towel.

4). Before cooking the potatoes, scrub them with a vegetable brush or a new scrubbing pad to clean them.

5). After cooking potatoes, add 1/4 cup vinegar or lemon juice to the water before draining them. Let the potatoes set for 10 minutes; this will keep them nice and white when you mash them.

6). To make a cheesy baked potato, take a cooked baked potato, cut across the top and pinch it open. Next scoop out about half of the potato, stuff it with grated cheddar cheese, 1 tablespoon butter, salt, and pepper to taste. Cover with the scooped out potato mixture. Add a little cheese on top.

7). To quickly bake potatoes, place them in a pan of water and boil them for 15 minutes. Drain the water and pat them dry with a paper towel. Pierce the skins and place them on a greased cookie sheet. Bake them in a preheated oven for 20 to 30 minutes until soft on the inside.

8). Herbs such as parsley, or chives can be chopped up and added to butter or sour cream and used on top of baked potatoes. Sprinkle paprika on top.

9). Leftover potatoes can be put in a zip lock baggie and frozen for future use.

10). Low fat sour cream or plain yogurt can be used as a substitute for regular sour cream if you are watching your fat intake.

11). Instant potatoes, pearls, flakes, or granules can be used for thickening in creamed soups or white sauces.

12). Avoid using soft, cut, bruised or sprouted potatoes. The sprouts, green spots and tops of the potatoes are toxic. Do not eat them or you might get sick. Just peel off the green spots before cooking them. If your potatoes have sprouted, break off the sprouts before cooking. Keep soft sprouted potatoes until springtime and plant them in your garden, they are considered seed potatoes and will have a head start.

13). Keep potatoes in a cool dark place, unwashed and open to the air for circulation. Do not refrigerate or let them freeze because the starch will turn to sugar and they will become sweet.

14). Never store your potatoes in the same place with your apples or onions; they will spoil each other.

15). Never plant tomatoes and potatoes in the same spot, they can cause each other diseases.

16). A sliced potato can be used as a compress on a wound to help draw out the toxins. Just wrap a slice of potato with gauze, tape it in place and leave it there for several hours.

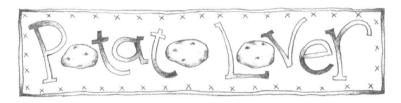

Dried Potato Products

1). There are several dried potato products on the market. They include: hash brown potatoes, potato slices, potato dices, potato flakes, potato pearls, and potato granules.

2). To reconstitute these products follow the manufactures instructions for each product. You can substitute these reconstituted potatoes in any recipe that calls for fresh potatoes.

3). The flakes, pearls, and granules can be reconstituted into fluffy mashed potatoes and used in any recipe calling for mashed potatoes. They have more salt than fresh potatoes do, so don't add as much salt to the recipe.

4). A simple way to reconstitute dried sliced, diced, and hash brown potatoes is to let them set until they are plump and have soaked up the water. If they look like they need more water, then add more. If there is excess water, just add the potatoes and water to your soups or drain them. You can cook them for 10 minutes to speed up the reconstitution process. If you want to use them for casseroles or to fry, drain the liquid off and pat them dry with a paper towel. Use them the same way you would fresh potatoes.

5). Potato pearls are my favorite. They taste wonderful and are so easy to prepare. For best results, follow the manufactures directions. It is usually 1 cup potato pearls to 2 cups boiling water with a little butter and salt added to the water. Stir continuously because they set up fast and you don't want any lumps. If the potatoes are a little stiff, just add small amounts of boiling water to the mixture and continue stirring until they are the consistency you want. If they are a little thin add a small amount of pearls to thicken them and continue stirring to prevent lumps. Use the manufactures directions, the instructions vary from product to product.

Funeral
Potatoes

POTATOES

20 LBS.

Introduction To Funeral Potatoes

Every geographic region and every group of people, whether religious or ethnic has its own traditional dishes, which become part of the groups' heritage. Funeral Potatoes are the ultimate comfort food and are usually associated with a funeral, family, church or social gathering.

Funeral Potatoes are such a dish. They can be found on the buffet table at every funeral luncheon, and just about every church social event. This is probably because it is an easy and inexpensive way to feed a lot of people.

For any gathering, Funeral Potatoes can be assigned to ten different people and you will get ten different variations. These potato recipes are loaded with fat grams, and calories. That's what makes this dish taste so wonderful.

Most of the recipes call for fresh or frozen hash browns, or boiled potatoes that have been cubed or sliced. Other main ingredients include canned cream of chicken, mushroom, or celery soup, sour cream, cheddar cheese, chopped green onions, spices, and a variety of toppings such as: corn flakes or Special K cereal, potato chips, corn flakes, french fried onion rings (in a can), bread or cracker crumbs. To finish off the topping, it is sprinkled with lots of cheese.

I recently attended a funeral. Of course, funeral potatoes were served at the luncheon. I overheard some of my relatives' comments on how delicious they were. We all had to try a sampling of several different casserole dishes.

The traditional recipes are all so simular. The names of these dishes usually describe the dish itself or one of the main ingredients. Some of the names I found include; Church or Ward Party Potatoes, Creamy Potluck Potatoes, Baked Potato Casserole, Scalloped Potatoes, Au-Gratin Potatoes, Sour Cream Potatoes, and Cheesy Potatoes.

These recipes have been handed down through families and church members. Many church groups have compiled cookbooks in which you will always find a recipe or two for funeral potatoes.

Amazing Traditional Funeral Potatoes
(This recipe is "Fabulous")

12 large potatoes boiled in their skins or a
(2 pound package) of frozen shredded hash
brown potatoes
2 Tablespoons melted butter
1 (10 oz) can cream of mushroom or chicken soup
1 (10 oz) soup can of milk
1 (16 oz) container sour cream
2 cups shredded cheddar cheese
6-8 green scallion onions with tops
1/4 teaspoon each garlic salt and onion salt
1/4 teaspoon dried parsley
1/2 teaspoon salt and 1/4 teaspoon pepper
Topping
Choose 2 cups of one of the following; Crushed
corn flakes, Special K cereal, potato chips,
french fried onion rings (in a can), bread or
cracker crumbs.
2 Tablespoons melted butter
2 Tablespoons Parmesan or cheddar cheese

1). Peel the skins off the boiled potatoes. Cut the potatoes onto thin
slices and layer them in a (9"x 13") baking dish. (Frozen hash brown
potatoes thawed, or reconstituted dehydrated hash browns can be
used instead of fresh potatoes).
2). Pour the melted butter over the potatoes.
3). In a medium sized mixing bowl stir together the cream soup, milk,
sour cream, cheese, onions, and seasonings.
4). Pour the mixture over the potatoes and gently mix together.
5). Bake in a preheated 350 degree oven for 20 minutes or until
mixture bubbles.
6). In a separate bowl combine (the topping of your choice) butter
and Parmesan or shredded cheddar cheese.
7). Sprinkle topping over potato mixture
and bake another 20 minutes until bubbly
and the crumbs are toasted. (Serves 12)

9

Au-Gratin Chicken and Potatoes

1 (10 oz) can of cream of chicken soup
3/4 cup sour cream
3/4 cup milk
1/2 teaspoon salt
2 cups chicken, cooked and cubed
2 cups shredded cheddar cheese
1 (32 oz) package frozen, hash brown potatoes
3/4 cup mixed vegetables
1/2 cup sour cream and onion potato chips
1/2 cup french fried onion rings

1). In a large bowl, combine soup, sour cream, milk, and salt. Stir in the chicken cubes and 1 & 1/2 cups cheese.
2). Add the hash brown potatoes and mixed vegetables. Stir well.
3). Put the potato mixture in a greased (9x13) casserole dish. Cover the dish with aluminum foil or a lid and bake at 350 degrees for 40 minutes, or until hot and bubbly.
4). Uncover and sprinkle remaining cheese on the top. Sprinkle crushed potato chips and french fried onion rings on top of the cheese. (French fried onion rings are found in the grocery store in the section with bread crumbs and other toppings. It comes in a can and is used as a topping on casseroles). Bake for 10-15 minutes longer until bubbly on top.
(Serves 8)

Au-Gratin Potatoes with Sausage

(This recipe is "Fabulous")

8 medium or large potatoes
1 pound smoked sausage
1 large onion, chopped
1 (10-oz) can of cream of chicken or
 mushroom soup
1 cup sour cream
1 cup evaporated milk
2 cups grated cheese
1/2 teaspoon salt
1/2 teaspoon pepper
1/2 teaspoon onion salt

1). Boil the potatoes in the skins. When they can be pierced with a fork they are done. Cool them in cold water.
2). Grease a casserole dish, peel, slice, or grate the potatoes in the dish. In a separate bowl mix all other ingredients together except onions and sausage. Put only half the amount of cheese into the mixture. Spread the sauce over the potato mixture and mix well.
3). Slice the sausage into round pieces about 1/4 inch thick. Fry it in a little butter along with the onions. If you are using regular sausage, fry, brown and crumble it first.
4). Add the onions and sausage to the potato mixture. Bake at 350 degrees for 30 minutes or until bubbly on top. The last 10 minutes of cooking , sprinkle the top with the remaining cheese and cook until it melts and turns slightly brown on top.
(Serves 8-10)

Buttermilk, Mushrooms, and Broccoli Au-Gratin

6 large Russet potatoes
2 & 1/2 Tablespoons butter
2 garlic cloves minced
2 shallots, minced
2 Tablespoons white flour
1 & 1/2 cups warm milk
1 cup buttermilk
1 teaspoon white pepper
1/4 cup mayonnaise
1 teaspoon Dijon mustard
1/2 teaspoon Worcestershire sauce
4 Tablespoons chopped fresh parsley
3 cups sliced mushrooms
1 (10 ounce) package frozen chopped broccoli
1 cup grated Monterey Jack cheese
1/4 cup crumbled blue cheese
2 cups crushed potato chips
1 Tablespoon diced pimento (canned)

1). Boil the potatoes in enough water to cover them. Cool and peel. Cut 1/8 inch round slices and arrange half of them in the bottom of a buttered casserole dish.
2). Make the sauce as follows: melt the butter in a saucepan over low heat. Add the garlic and shallots and cook until they are translucent. Add the flour and stir. Continue cooking until it thickens. Add the milk and buttermilk all at once. Stir continuously until the sauce thickens and bubbles. Remove from the heat and stir in all ingredients except the Monterey Jack cheese, blue cheese, potato chips, and pimento.
3). Pour half the sauce on the potatoes and sprinkle half of the cheese over the top. Layer the other potatoes, sauce, and cheese.
4). Bake for 45 minutes at 350 degrees. Sprinkle the crushed potato chips, Monterey Jack cheese, blue cheese, and the pimento on top. Bake for another 10 minutes.
(Serves 6)

Cheesy Layered Potatoes

(Using dried foods)

3 cups dried potato slices
6 cups water
1/2 teaspoon salt
1 cup powdered milk
2 & 1/4 cups water
1/4 cup butter powder
1/4 cup all purpose flour
1/2 cup cheddar cheese blend powder
2/3 cup bacon bits

1). Boil the dried potatoes in the 6 cups of water with salt.
2). When the potatoes are tender, drain and set aside.
3). To make the sauce, mix all remaining ingredients together (except bacon bits) until lumps are dissolved. Cook in a sauce pan and continue stirring until the sauce thickens.
4). In a small casserole dish, layer the potatoes, sauce, and bacon bits at least two layers thick.
5). Pour all the remaining sauce over the top.
6). Place in the oven and bake at 350 degrees for 30 minutes, until golden brown and bubbly on top.
(Serves 6)

Cheesy Scalloped Potatoes

(This recipe is "Fabulous")

6 potatoes cooked, cooled, and peeled
12 slices of bacon, cooked and crumbled
1/2 cup sliced green scallion onions with tops
3 Tablespoons butter
2 Tablespoons all-purpose flour
2 cups half and half or cream
1 clove of garlic, crushed
1 bay leaf
1/4 teaspoon each of salt, pepper, and celery seeds
1 & 1/2 cups or (6 oz.) cheddar cheese shredded.

1). Peel the potatoes and cut them into slices about 1/4 inch thick.
2). Cook the potatoes in boiling water for about 5-7 minutes until tender. Layer the potatoes in a (9x13) inch baking dish.
3). Sprinkle the crumbled bacon and scallion onions over the potatoes. Set aside.
4). Melt the butter in a heavy saucepan over low heat. Slowly add flour, stirring well. Cook about 1 minute, stirring constantly to prevent clumping.
5). Gradually add the half and half or cream. Cook over medium heat, stirring constantly until mixture is slightly thickened and bubbly. Add garlic, spices, and cheese, until the cheese melts. Remove the bay leaf and throw it away.
6). Pour the cheesy mixture over the top of the layered potato slices. Cover the dish with foil or a lid and bake at 350 degrees for 30 minutes. Remove cover, and bake an additional 15 minutes until the top is golden brown.
(Serves 6)

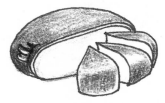

14

French Potatoes Au-Gratin

2 pounds or 8 large potatoes
1 & 1/2 teaspoons salt
1/8 teaspoon black pepper
Dash of grated nutmeg
2 cloves minced garlic
1 & 3/4 cups whipping cream or half and half

1). Peel the potatoes and cut them in 1/4 inch slices.
2). Grease a (9x13) inch casserole dish. Layer the potatoes in the dish, alternating the salt, pepper, nutmeg and garlic in between the layers of potato.
3). Pour the cream over the potato mixture. Sprinkle a little nutmeg on top for color.
4). Bake at 400 degrees F. for about 40 minutes or until the potato casserole is tender and the top is golden brown. (Serves 6-8)

Julian Potatoes Cooked in Cream

(This recipe is "Fabulous")

4 large potatoes
5 Tablespoons butter
3 Tablespoons flour
2 teaspoons dry mustard
1 & 3/4 cups milk or cream
1/4 teaspoon salt
1/8 teaspoon pepper
1/8 teaspoon onion
1/8 teaspoon garlic powder
1/2 teaspoon dried or fresh parsley
1 & 1/2 cups grated cheddar cheese

1). Preheat oven to 400 degrees. Grease an ovenproof casserole dish with 2 tablespoons of the butter.
2). Peel the potatoes and cut them into french fries. Place the potatoes in a saucepan with water to cover and bring to a boil. Cook the potatoes until they are almost tender. About 2 minutes.
3). Melt the remaining butter in a saucepan and stir in the flour. Add the mustard and milk and stir constantly until it comes to a boil. Reduce the heat and simmer for 2 minutes, then add salt and pepper, onion, and garlic powder, and parsley.
4). Pour the sauce over the potatoes. Sprinkle cheese on top. Bake for 20 minutes or until golden brown on top.
(Serves 4)

Parmesan and Fennel Scalloped Potatoes

6 small potatoes or 2 pounds
1 & 1/2 cups heavy cream
1 cup whole milk
1/4 cup chopped chives
1 Tablespoon fresh, chopped tarragon
1 teaspoon fresh, chopped thyme
1 teaspoon salt
1/2 teaspoon pepper
1 fennel bulb, with stalk removed
1 cup freshly grated Parmesan cheese

1). Preheat the oven to 400 degrees. Grease or butter a small baking dish (8 inch). Boil the potatoes in enough water to cover. Cook until barely tender. Cool, peel and slice them to about 1/8 inch thickness.

2). Slice the fennel into quarters then again into 1/8 inch pieces including 3-4 tablespoons of the green tops. Set aside.

3). In another cooking pot, make the cream sauce by combining cream, milk, chives, tarragon, thyme, salt, and pepper. Add the sliced potatoes to the mixture. Bring this mixture to a boil for 1 minute. Add the fennel including the green tops. Stir often. Boil for about 2 more minutes.

4). Place half the potato mixture in the baking dish. Sprinkle half the Parmesan cheese over the top. Layer the remaining mixture and top it with the remaining cheese. Cover the dish with a oven proof cover or aluminum foil.

5). Bake in the oven for 45 minutes or until the top is bubbling. Remove the foil or lid and bake another 20 minutes until the top is golden brown, the potatoes are tender, and the sauce is thick.
(Serves 6)

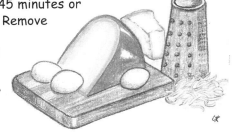

Scalloped French Fries

1/2 cup butter
3/4 cup chopped green pepper
1/2 cup chopped celery
1 medium onion
1/2 cup flour
1 & 1/2 teaspoons salt
1/4 teaspoon pepper
Onion salt and celery salt to taste
4 cups milk
1/3 cup chopped pimento
3/4 cup coarsely shredded carrots
3 (9-oz) packages frozen french fries
3/4 pound shredded processed or cheddar cheese.

1). Melt the butter in a large cooking skillet. Add the vegetables and cook until tender.
2). Blend in the flour, salt, and pepper. stir to remove any lumps in the flour mixture.
3). Gradually add the milk a little at a time. Cook and stir until the mixture is thick.
4). Add the pimentos, carrots, potatoes, and half the shredded cheese. Pour into 2 (9 x13) casserole dishes. Bake for 30 minutes at 375 degrees.
5). Sprinkle with cheese and bake 5 more minutes.
(Serves 12)

18

Scalloped Potatoes and Ham

6 medium potatoes peeled and sliced
3 Tablespoons butter
3 Tablespoons white flour
1 & 1/2 cups milk, half and half or cream
8 ounces of cheese
1 & 1/2 cups of diced ham

1). Boil the potatoes in enough water to cover them. When they are tender, drain them and run cold water over them to cool.
2). To prepare the white sauce, melt the butter in a saucepan and stir in the flour. Cook for about 30 seconds until blended. Slowly add the milk or cream. Evaporated milk is also very good to use. When the white sauce thickens, add the cheese.
3). Place the potatoes and ham alternately in a (9x13) inch baking dish.
4). Place the white sauce on top of the potato mixture and bake at 350 degrees for one hour or until the potatoes are golden brown and bubbly on top.

(Serves 6)

Sour Cream Scalloped Potatoes

(Using frozen hash brown potatoes)
(This recipe is "Fabulous")

1 lb. package of frozen hash browns
1 (10 oz can) of cream of chicken soup
1 cup of sour cream
8 ounces of grated cheddar cheese
1/2 medium onion chopped in small pieces
1 & 1/2 cups corn flakes
1/2 cube butter

1). Combine all ingredients except corn flakes and butter. Place in a casserole dish.
2). Melt the butter. Mix the corn flakes and butter together. Sprinkle on the top of the potatoes.
3). Bake at 350 degrees for 45 minutes or until the mixture bubbles and browns on top.
(Serves 8-10)

20

Spinach and Feta, Potato Casserole

(This recipe is "Fabulous")

2 pounds or 8 large potatoes
1 cup plain yogurt
2 Tablespoons butter
1/2 teaspoon salt
1/8 teaspoon cayenne pepper
2 eggs, beaten
1 cup feta cheese with herbs
1/4 cup water
1 (10-ounce) package of fresh spinach
1/4 teaspoon paprika

1). Peel the potatoes and cut them up into quarters.

2). Place the quartered potatoes in a saucepan and cover with water. Boil the potatoes until they are tender. About 20 minutes.

3). Drain the potatoes and mash with a potato masher, or an electric mixer. Eight cups of instant mashed potatoes may be substituted for the 8 potatoes.

4). Add the yogurt, butter, salt, and cayenne pepper.

5). Slightly beat the potato mixture, adding the eggs a little at a time and beating for 1 minute.

6). Fold in half of the feta cheese. Set the rest of the mixture aside.

7). In a saucepan bring the 1/4 cup water to a full boil and add the spinach. Cook the spinach until it starts to wilt. Drain the water and get out as much liquid as possible. Chop the spinach.

8). Using a greased (9x13) inch casserole dish. Layer half the potato mixture, then the spinach and feta cheese. Spread remaining potato mixture on top of the spinach and feta cheese. Top it off with a sprinkle of paprika for color.

9). Bake in an oven preheated to 425 degrees for about 15 minutes or until it is golden brown on top. (Serves 8)

Baked Potatoes

Low Fat Substitutions and Potato Toppings

Sour Cream Substitute
In a blender combine 1 cup low fat yogurt and 1 cup low fat cottage cheese. Blend until smooth. Use this to replace sour cream. If this is heated, it tends to separate a little, so use it only in recipes that are not heated.

Low Fat Ideas
If all those fat grams swimming around on the baked potatoes and casseroles scare you, here are some ideas to lower the fat intake.

1). Instead of using butter, use a substitute called "I can't believe it's not butter".

2). You can purchase low fat cheese in different flavors to put on top of any of the following combinations.

3). Chop 2 tomatoes and 2 green onions together, sprinkle balsamic vinegar on them until they are well coated. Put this on the top of a baked potato. Add chopped chives or parsley.

4). Make a gravy out of "au-jus" or natural juices from chicken bouillon. Add a little flour or corn starch mixed with a little water to the au-jus to thicken it. Season to taste with salt and pepper. If it becomes too thick add more juice. If it is too thin add a little more thickener mixed with water.

5). Use pace picante sauce or salsa on top of the potato and add a dab of sour cream substitute on top of a baked potato.

6). Stir fry (enough for one person) chopped broccoli and asparagus together until tender. Add 2-3 tablespoons of cream cheese until it melts. Put this on top of a baked potato.

7). Stir fry mushrooms, green peppers and sliced onions together and cook until caramelized or (see through). Put this on top of a baked potato.

8). Fry one sliced chicken breast with your favorite sliced vegetables (however much you want) and 2 cloves garlic. Add 1/2 cup cooked pasta per person to the mixture, add salt and pepper to taste. Put this mixture on top of a baked potato and sprinkle with low fat cheese. Bake just until the cheese melts.

9). Slice up Portobello mushrooms to equal 2 cups. Add 2 tablespoons chopped garlic bulbs add 1 teaspoon Worcestershire sauce, 1/2 teaspoon sugar, and 2 tablespoons chopped oysters with sauce. Add salt and pepper to taste and any other favorite herbs. Add 1 cup half and half cream and 1 tablespoon of cornstarch together and mix well. Pour over the mixture and cook until thick.

Baked Potato Bar

One baked potato per person
Butter
Sour cream
Ranch dressing
Salt and pepper
Shredded cheddar or mozzarella cheese
Sliced scallion onions
Chives (chopped)
Sliced olives
Sliced mushrooms
Frozen peas (thawed)
Chopped broccoli
Cooked kidney or red beans
Chili
Crumbled bacon or bacon bits
Chopped ham
Chunks of chicken
Cream of chicken soup made into gravy
Crumbled ground beef
Beef gravy

To set up a baked Potato bar you need to put several of the following items in bowls and let each person take a baked potato, cut it across the top and open it up so it can be filled with the items listed. Sprinkle cheese on top. It is very delicious and feeds a large crowd.

Baked Potatoes in a Crockpot

6-8 large potatoes
Tin Foil

1). Prick or puncture each potato by stabbing it in several places with a fork or a knife.

2). Rub vegetable oil on the skins of the potatoes before wrapping them in tin foil.

3). Fill the crockpot with the potatoes wrapped in foil. Cover the crockpot and turn it on high for 3-4 hours. Do not add any water. These potatoes are meant to be cooked dry. The potatoes are done when you can insert a knife into the center and the potato is tender. The bigger the potatoes the longer it will take to cook them. These potatoes come out just right every time.

Microwave Baked Potatoes

1). The best method of baking a potato in the microwave is to cut the potato down the center so the steam can escape. Place the potato in a zip lock baggie. Do not seal the bag because it needs to be vented.

2). Another way to do it is to poke holes in the potatoes. Wrap a potato in a wet paper towel and place in the microwave. Cook 5-7 minutes on high. Take the potato out of the microwave, remove the paper towel and wrap it in tin foil, and Let the potato cool down for 7-10 more minutes.

3). The potatoes will bake better if they are wrapped. The microwave is heating the moisture in the potato and cooking it from the inside out with steam produced inside the potato. The potato must be vented or it will not cook evenly, and it must set for a few minutes after it is cooked.

Perfect Baked Potatoes in the Oven

To make the potato crispy on the outside and tender and fluffy on the inside, pierce the entire outside of the potato and rub it with butter or oil, sprinkle salt on the outside and cook it on a baking rack in the center of the oven for one hour.

To make the outside soft and the inside fluffy and tender, pierce the outside of the potato with a fork, rub butter or oil on it, then wrap the potato in tin foil and bake in the oven for 1 hour.

4 large baking potatoes
Butter
Salt and Pepper to taste
Paprika for color
4-6 Tablespoons sour cream
Crumbled Bacon (6-8) pieces
Chopped green scallion onions

1). Preheat the oven to 425 degrees.
2). Wash the potatoes well and dry them thoroughly. Puncture the skins of the entire potato with a fork.
3). Oil or butter the skins of the potatoes and place the potatoes on an oven rack, (or wrap them in tin foil). Bake 1 hour or until they can be pierced easily with a fork.
4). Slash an x on the top of the potato lengthwise and squeeze the potato so the steam can escape and the potato fluffs up.
5). Add a pat of butter to the center, sprinkle salt, pepper, and paprika. Top with a tablespoon of sour cream, crumbled bacon, and onions.
6). Another great variation includes warm chili over the potato with cheese on top.
(Serves 4)

Red Potato Boats with Goat Cheese

12 new red potatoes
3 Tablespoons olive oil
Salt and pepper to taste
1 pound of goat or feta cheese crumbled
1/4 cup toasted pine nuts
1/4 cup sun dried tomatoes packed in oil,
drained, patted dry and chopped
1/4 cup green olives, chopped
2 Tablespoons chives
2 Tablespoons parsley

1). Preheat the oven to 350 degrees. Toss the potatoes in the olive oil to coat them. Sprinkle the salt and pepper on them and place them in a baking dish and roast them in the oven for 20-30 minutes until they are cooked all the way through.
2). Remove the potatoes from the oven and let them cool a little. Cut the potatoes in half. Scoop out about one teaspoon of the potato centers to create a potato boat. Use the leftover potato for something else or eat it separately.
3). Fill each potato boat with the goat cheese, pine nuts, sun dried tomatoes, and olives.
4). Place the potato boats on a platter and garnish the tops of them with chopped chives and parsley. Serve warm.
(Serves 12)

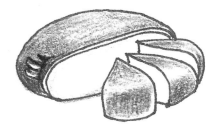

Spinach and Cheddar
Twice Baked Potatoes

6 large Russet or Idaho potatoes
8 Tablespoons butter
3 large cloves garlic
1 large shallot, chopped fine
3-4 cups fresh spinach
3 Tablespoons sour cream
Salt and pepper to taste
1 & 1/2 cups finely shredded cheddar cheese

1). Preheat the oven to 400 degrees. Wash and stem the spinach, cut it in strips and set aside. Puncture the potatoes with a fork or knife in several places . Place them on the middle oven rack and cook them for 1 hour or until they are tender. Remove them from the rack and let them cool. Reduce the oven temperature to 350 degrees.

2). In a large cooking pot, melt 3 tablespoons butter on medium or low heat. Add the garlic and shallots and saute' until they are tender. Raise the heat to medium and add the washed and steamed spinach. Cook until the spinach wilts. Remove from heat and set aside.

3). Take the baked potatoes and cut a lengthwise strip across the top. Scoop out all the baked potato from all 6 potatoes. Put mixture in a medium bowl. Leave the potato skin 1/4 inch thick and in tact to be used later. To the potato, add sour cream, salt, pepper, and remaining butter. Mash the potato mixture until it looks like creamy mashed potatoes. Next add the spinach and 3/4 cup of cheese, mix well.

4). Divide the mixture into 6 equal parts. Spoon the potato mixture into the shells and mound it. Sprinkle 1 tablespoon of cheese on top of each potato boat.

5). Place the potatoes on a baking sheet and bake in the preheated 350 degree oven for 20-25 minutes. Serve them hot. (Serves 6)

Twice Baked Potatoes

6 large baking potatoes
2 Tablespoons butter
1 teaspoon salt
1/4 teaspoon pepper
1/4 teaspoon parsley
1/4 cup hot milk
1/4 cup sour cream
Shredded cheddar cheese for topping

1). Preheat the oven to 425 degrees.
2). Wash the potatoes well and dry them thoroughly. Puncture the skins of the entire potato with a fork.
3). Place the potatoes on an oven rack, (or wrap them in tin foil). Bake for 1 hour or until they can be pierced easily, and feel soft.
4). Cut the potatoes lengthwise in half. Scoop out the middle of each shell, being careful not to break the shell.
5). Put the potato in a bowl and add butter, salt, pepper, parsley, hot milk and sour cream. Beat the mixture until it is fluffy. Divide the mixture into 6 equal parts. Fill the shells until they are heaping full. Top with shredded cheese. Melt the cheese. (Serves 4-6)

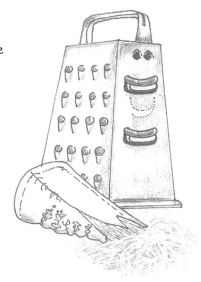

Tin Foil Baked Potatoes

1 potato per person
1 Tablespoon butter
1 Tablespoon minced onion
Salt and pepper to taste
1/2 cup ground beef cooked and crumbled
Tin foil (8x8 inch sheet per person)

1). Wash and peel the potatoes. Slice them up and place them in the center of a sheet of tin foil. Place butter, onion, and ground beef over the potatoes. Salt and pepper the tops.
2). Pull the edges of the foil up and seal all sides like a pouch. Cook the foil pouches on a barbeque or grill over a camp fire for 25-30 minutes. Until the potatoes are tender.

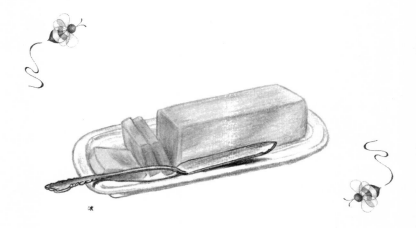

Breads

Mashed Potato Bread

(Using dried potato flakes)

1/2 lb. or 4 med. sized potatoes or (1 & 1/2
cups potato flakes, reconstituted with 3 cups
boiling water)
1 pkg. active dry yeast
1 Tablespoon sugar
1/4 cube butter melted
2 teaspoons salt
9 cups all purpose flour

1). Peel and cut the potatoes into quarters.
2). In a saucepan, cover the potatoes with a quart of water
and boil them until they are tender.
3). Drain off the water into a bowl and save the potato water.
Cool it to room temperature. If you are using dried potatoes,
mix 3 tablespoons dried potatoes to 3 cups warm water to
make potato water.
4). Mix 3 cups warm potato water, yeast, and sugar together
and allow to stand for 5 minutes to let the yeast grow.
5). Mash the potatoes, butter, and salt together
6). Combine the Potato mixture with half the flour. Keep
adding a little more flour, until it clings together and forms a
dough. If the dough is sticky, add a little extra flour until the
dough clings to itself and forms a ball.
7). Kneed the dough on a floured counter top or surface
for 5 minutes.
8). Allow the dough to rest for 10 minutes
9). Punch the dough down and continue kneading it until it is
smooth. You can add a little flour to the counter as you knead
the dough to keep it from sticking.
10). Make a ball with the dough and put a little cooking oil on
the surface to keep it from drying out. Place it in a large covered bowl and let it stand in a warm area until the dough doubles. This takes about 45 minutes.
11). Punch down the dough and knead it for a few minutes.

12). Divide the dough in half. Shape it into 2 loaves or two round balls. Place it in bread pans for regular loaves and on a cookie sheet for round loaves. Let it rise another 45 minutes or until the dough doubles in size.

13). Preheat the oven to 350 degrees. Bake for 40-45 minutes.

14). Remove the loaves from the pan immediately after baking and allow the bread to cool on a baking rack before cutting it. This prevents it from going soggy on the bottom. Serve with butter. (Makes 2 loaves)

Mashed Potato Refrigerator Rolls

(Using dried potato flakes)

1/2 cup instant potato flakes
1 cup boiling water
1/3 cup shortening
1 teaspoon salt
2 eggs
1 package instant yeast
1/2 cup warm water
1/4 cup sugar
1 cup scalded milk, cooled (or use 1/3 cup dry milk mixed with 1 cup boiling water)
6-8 cups flour

1). Prepare instant mashed potatoes by mixing with 1 cup of boiling water.
2). Add shortening, salt, and eggs. Mix well.
3). Dissolve yeast in 1/2 cup lukewarm water. Add the sugar. Add the milk after it has cooled down to room temperature.
4). Add the mashed potato mixture. Mix well and let it set for 10 minutes.
5). Add the flour a cup at a time until a dough forms. If the dough is still sticky, keep adding a little flour at a time until the dough sticks to itself. If the dough is becoming stiff then don't add all the flour.
6). Flour the counter top and knead the dough until it is smooth.
7). Place the dough in a large bowl and let it rise until double in size.
8). Rub the dough with oil to coat the entire surface.
9). Cover the bowl tightly and put it in the refrigerator.
10). Remove 1 & 1/2 hours before baking time. Pinch off roll size pieces of dough. Place on a baking sheet or roll pan. Let the rolls rise until double.
11). Bake in a preheated oven at 400 degrees for 15-20 minutes.
12). When the tops of the rolls are slightly brown, brush them with melted butter. Cook a few more minutes until the tops of the rolls are golden brown. (Makes 18 rolls)

Mashed Potato Waffles

(Using dried potato flakes)

1 cup flour
1/3 cup potato flakes
2 teaspoons sugar
2 teaspoons baking powder
1/2 teaspoon salt
2 eggs
1 & 1/2 cups milk
1 Tablespoon salad oil

1). In a large bowl, mix flour, potato flakes, sugar, baking powder, and salt.
2). In another bowl beat together eggs, milk, and oil. Add to dry ingredients and mix well.
3). Drop batter on waffle iron and cook until golden brown.
4). Top with fresh fruit, honey, butter, syrup, or jam.
(Serves 6)

Melt in Your Mouth Potato Rolls

(Using dried potato flakes)

3 & 1/2 cups all purpose white flour
1 package active dry yeast
3/4 cup water
1/2 cup half and half or milk
1/3 cup shortening
1/4 cup sugar
1 teaspoon salt
1/3 cup mashed potato flakes (instant)
1 egg

1). In a large bowl mix together the flour and yeast.
2). In a separate saucepan heat the water, milk, shortening, sugar, and salt until barely warm and the shortening starts to melt.
3). Stir in the potato flakes. Let it stand for 1 minute to become fluffy.
4). Add the potato mixture to the dry mixture along with the egg. Beat with an electric mixer until all the flour is mixed in. Approximately 3 minutes. Use a wooden spoon if necessary.
5). Place dough onto a floured surface or countertop. Knead the dough, adding a little flour if necessary, until it is smooth and elastic.
6). Shape the dough into a ball. Grease the ball and place in a large bowl. Cover with plastic wrap and let it rise about 1 hour and 15 minutes, or until the dough is double in size.
7). Punch the dough down and divide it in half. Place each half separately on a floured surface. Let it rise again for 15 minutes. Lightly grease two casserole dishes, or baking pans.
8). Knead each portion of bread dough and pinch off (2 inch x 2 inch) portions, and roll each one into a ball. Place the balls close together in the baking dish. Let them rise again until double.
9). Bake in a preheated oven at 375 degrees for 15 to 20 minutes or until golden brown on top. Remove the rolls from the oven while they are still warm. Cool them on a wire rack.
(Makes 24 rolls)

Potato Biscuits

2 medium potatoes or 1 & 1/2 cups peeled and
cooked potatoes
1 & 1/2 cups flour
2 Tablespoons baking powder
2 teaspoons salt
2 Tablespoons butter
6 Tablespoons milk

1). Put the potatoes through a ricer or mash them, set aside.
2). In a large bowl, stir together flour, baking powder and salt.
With a pastry cutter, or two knives, cut in the butter until it
resembles little pea shaped granules.
3). Stir in the potato, then the milk, blending lightly with a
fork.
4). Drop spoonfuls of biscuit dough onto a greased baking
sheet.
5). Bake at 400 degrees for 15 minutes or until golden brown.
(Serves 10)

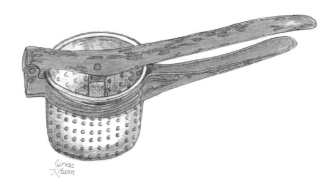

Potato Pancakes

(Using dried or fresh hash browns)

**3 cups grated potatoes or 3 cups reconstituted
dried hash browns
2 eggs beaten
3 Tablespoons flour
1/2 teaspoon baking powder
1 teaspoon salt
1 finely chopped apple (optional)**

1). Peel potatoes and grate them. Wash and dry them thoroughly. If dried potatoes are used, reconstitute them first by
adding 1 & 1/2 cups dried hash brown potatoes to 3 cups warm
water. Let them soak up the water completely. Add the eggs
to the potatoes and stir. Add remaining ingredients
and mix well.
2). In a hot oiled skillet, pour the batter into pancake sized
portions. Brown well on one side and turn over to brown on the
other side.
3). Serve with applesauce or fruit on top.
(Serves 4)

Sweet Potato Pancakes

1 medium sweet potato
1 & 1/3 cups all-purpose flour
3 Tablespoons sugar
2 teaspoons baking powder
3/4 teaspoon sea salt
1/4 teaspoon ground ginger
1 cup buttermilk
2 large eggs
1 Tablespoon butter

1). Peel the sweet potato and cut it in fourths. Place the potato quarters in a saucepan and boil until just tender. Put the potatoes in the refrigerator to cool them down.
2). When the sweet potato quarters are cooled down they need to be grated with the largest grater you have.
3). Mix the flour, sugar, baking powder, salt, and ginger. Add the buttermilk, beaten eggs, and 1 tablespoon melted butter. Mix well. Add the grated sweet potato. Mix well again.
4). Put a small amount of oil or butter in a heavy frying pan. Pour 1/2 cup of batter into the pan for each pancake. Fry on one side until brown and flip it over and cook on the other side until it is brown. Continue cooking pancakes until they are all cooked.
5). Serve with honey butter and syrup.
(Serves 6)

Sweet Potato Bread

1 & 1/2 cups sweet potatoes, peeled and cubed
Enough water to cover the potatoes for boiling
2/3 cup room temperature water
4 Tablespoons sugar or 2 Tablespoons honey
2 Tablespoons vegetable oil
3 Tablespoons fresh squeezed orange juice
1 orange rind grated
2 & 1/2 cups all purpose bread flour
1 Tablespoon active dry yeast
1 teaspoon ground cinnamon
5 Tablespoons butter

1). Boil the sweet potatoes in the water until tender. Drain the water and mash them until they are smooth.
2). In a large bowl combine the water, sugar or honey, oil, orange juice and rind.
3). Add the mashed sweet potatoes, half of the flour, and the remaining ingredients. Mix until it forms a sticky dough. Let the dough set for 10 minutes to activate the yeast.
4). Cut the butter into small pieces and mix it into the dough with the remaining flour. Knead it until it forms a smooth dough. If it is too sticky add small amounts of flour, a little at a time to form a smooth dough.
5). Grease a regular sized bread pan. Form the dough into a loaf and place it in the pan. Put it in a warm place and cover it until the dough doubles in size.
6). Bake at 375 degrees for 45-60 minutes. The bread is done when a knife inserted into the
center comes out clean.
Take the bread out of
the pan and let it
cool on a wire rack.
(Makes 1 loaf)

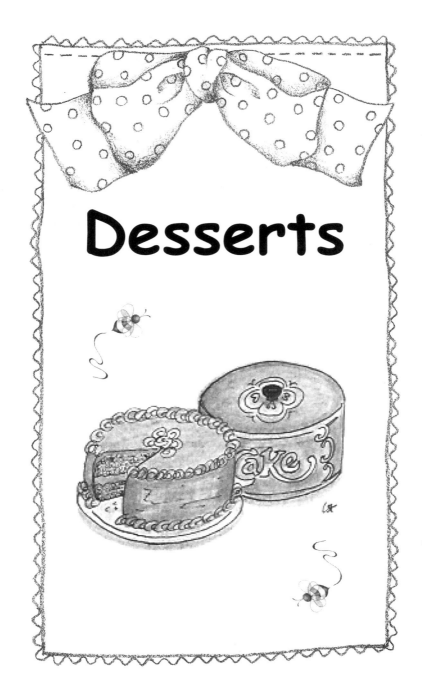

Desserts

Mashed Potato Chocolate Cake

(Using dried potato flakes)

1 cup softened butter
2 cups sugar
4 eggs
2 cups flour
1/2 tsp salt
2 teaspoons baking powder
1 teaspoon each, cloves and cinnamon
1/4 teaspoon nutmeg
4 Tablespoons grated chocolate
1 cup mashed potatoes or (1/2 cup potato flakes
or pearls reconstituted with 1 cup boiling water).
1/2 cup milk or cream
1 cup chopped nuts
1 teaspoon vanilla

1). Cream butter, sugar, and eggs. Mix well.
2). Sift the flour, salt, baking powder, and spices together.
Add the chocolate.
3). If you are using potato flakes, add the boiling water first,
stir until mixture is light and fluffy or mash fresh potatoes.
In a separate bowl mix the milk and mashed potatoes. Combine
all ingredients and mix well. Add the nuts and vanilla. Place
the batter in a greased bunt pan. Bake
in a preheated oven at 350
degrees for 45 minutes.
(Serves 12)

Potato Apple Crisp

(Using dried potato granules)

4 apples peeled and sliced
2/3 cup potato granules
4 Tablespoons sugar
6 Tablespoons brown sugar
1/2 teaspoon cinnamon
3 Tablespoons butter

1). Cook the peeled apples in a saucepan with enough water to cover them. When they are partially cooked, Arrange the apple slices in a non-stick or greased (8 x13) inch baking dish.
2). In another bowl combine remaining ingredients. Cut in the butter with a pastry cutter or two knives until it resembles pea sized granules.
3). Sprinkle mixture over apples.
4). Bake, uncovered, at 375 degrees for 25 minutes or until apples are tender.
(Serves 6)

Potato and Coconut Cookies

1 cup softened butter
1 cup sugar or 1/2 cup honey
1 egg
1/4 cup coconut flakes
1 teaspoon baking soda
1 & 3/4 cups flour
1 & 1/2 cups instant potato flakes

1). Combine butter, sugar or honey, and egg together and beat the mixture until smooth.
2). Add the remaining ingredients. Drop by teaspoonfuls on a greased cookie sheet. Bake at 325 degrees for 10-12 minutes. (Makes 15-20 cookies)

Spud Nuts or Idaho (Donuts)

1 pound potatoes, boiled, peeled, and mashed
2 packages instant active dry yeast
1 & 1/2 cups lukewarm potato water
1/2 cup melted butter or vegetable oil
1/2 cup sugar
2 large or 3 small eggs
1 teaspoon salt
7 & 1/2 cups all purpose flour
Vegetable oil for deep frying the donuts
Vanilla frosting mix or frosting of your choice

1). Boil the potatoes, save the potato water, peel them and place in a bowl with a small amount of milk to moisten them. Mash until they are light and fluffy. Set aside.
2). In a separate bowl combine the yeast and warm potato water. If the liquid is too hot it could kill the yeast. Let it set for 10 minutes to activate the yeast. Add the mashed potatoes to the yeast and stir.
3). In a separate bowl combine the butter or oil, sugar, eggs, and salt together. Mix this with the potato, yeast water. Add the flour a cup at a time and stir until it forms a dough. If it is sticky, continue adding a small amount of flour until a dough forms. You may not need all the flour.
4). Let the dough rise until it is double in size (about 35 minutes)
5). On a floured surface, roll the dough out to about 1 inch thick. Use a donut cutter or a biscuit cutter. If you do not have a donut cutter and you use a biscuit cutter, you can find something small and round to cut out the center of the donut.
6). Fry the spud nuts in hot vegetable oil. Fry on one side, then turn them over and fry to a golden brown on the other side. Put them on a paper towel to absorb the oil and let them cool a little.
7). Any kind of frosting can be used to drizzle over the top of the donut. Dip them in chocolate or colored sprinkles. For variation you can dip them in powdered sugar or cinnamon sugar mixture.
8). Make a glaze out of 4 cups of powdered sugar, 1/3 cup of water, and 1 teaspoon vanilla. Or use your imagination to glaze them. Mix well. (Makes 48)

Superb Spud Bars

(Dried potato flakes or pearls)

> I am from Idaho and I was always called a spud when I went to college. That is a nickname for someone from Idaho, it's also a nickname for a potato.

2 Tablespoons butter
1/2 cup granulated sugar
1/4 cup packed brown sugar
1/2 cup flour
1/2 teaspoon baking soda
1/4 teaspoon salt
1/4 teaspoon cinnamon
1 egg
1 teaspoon vanilla extract
1/2 cup potato flakes of pearls
1/2 cup chocolate chips

1). In a large bowl cream together butter and sugars.
2). Beat in the flour, soda, cinnamon, and salt. Stir in the remaining ingredients. Mix well.
4). Pour the batter into a square (8 inch) greased baking pan.
5). Bake at 350 degrees for 20 minutes.
6). Cut the bars into 16 (2 inch squares).
(Serves 16)

Fried Potatoes

French Fried Potatoes

Long White or Russet potatoes make the best French fries.
Salad oil or shortening for frying

1). Peel as many potatoes as you desire. Cut them into shoe-string sticks about 1/2 inch thick and about 3 inches long. Rinse the french fries in cold water to remove the starch and thoroughly dry them on paper towels.
2). Pour the oil or shortening into a deep fat fryer approximately 3/4 full, or use a deep heavy gauge pan. Heat the deep-fat fryer to 360 degrees on the fryer thermometer.
3). Fry the potatoes in the oil until they are golden brown and cooked thoroughly. Remove the wire basket and let the oil drain. Place the french fries on a paper towel and pat with another piece of paper towel to remove the oil.
4). Sprinkle with salt and keep warm until served.
(1 potato serves 1 person)

French Fry Sauce

1/2 cup mayonnaise
1/4 cup ketchup

1). Mix together until well blended.

Garlic and Rosemary Oven Fried Potatoes

4 large baking potatoes
1/4 cup water
1 Tablespoon olive oil
2 teaspoons dried crushed rosemary
2 cloves minced garlic
1/2 teaspoon salt
1/2 teaspoon paprika
1/4 teaspoon pepper

1). Quarter the potatoes with the skins on.
2). Combine all remaining ingredients
3). Add the potatoes to the oil and spice mixture, coat all sides of the potatoes. (Save remaining sauce).
4). Place the potatoes in a shallow baking dish and bake in the oven on 400 degrees for 30-40 minutes or until tender and golden brown.
5). After about 20 minutes. Turn the potatoes so all sides will be browned. Coat the potatoes with more sauce. Continue baking until golden brown on all sides.

(Serves 5)

Hash Brown Breakfast Cake

1 & 1/2 pounds or 4-5 medium potatoes
2 Tablespoons minced fresh parsley
1 clove garlic, crushed
Salt and pepper to taste
2 Tablespoons butter
1 Tablespoon oil
1/2 cup Parmesan cheese

1). Wash potatoes and place them in a saucepan with water to cover. Boil until the potatoes are tender but still firm.
2). Cool the potatoes down sufficiently so you can work with them. Peel the potatoes and grate them into a big bowl. Mix in parsley, garlic, salt and pepper to taste.
3). In a nonstick 7-8 inch skillet, heat the butter and oil together. Divide and form the potato mixture into 8 patties. Fry each one until it is golden brown. Flip it over in the frying pan and fry the other side.
4). Sprinkle the top with parmesan cheese and serve it hot.
(Serves 8)

Hash Brown Potato Pie

(Using dried hash browns)

6 cups shredded frozen hash browns, 6 cups fresh shredded, or (3 cups dried hash browns reconstituted with 6 cups hot water)
1 cup butter melted
2 cups cooked ham (chopped)
2 cups cheddar cheese
2/3 cup chopped green pepper
8 eggs or (8 Tablespoons dried egg powder mixed with 8 Tablespoons water)
1/4 cup powdered milk
1 cup water
Salt and pepper to taste

1). If you are reconstituting dehydrated hash browns, drain the liquid and pat them dry with a paper towel.
2). If you are using fresh potatoes, boil them, let them cool, and shred them into hash browns.
3). Grease a (9 x 13) casserole dish. Press the hash browns onto the bottom and up the sides of the dish. Drizzle 1/2 cup butter all over the potatoes. Bake at 425 degrees for 30 minutes.
4). Combine remaining ingredients together in a bowl and pour it into the potato crust.
5). Bake the pie at 350 degrees for 30 more minutes. Let it cool.
(Serves 8)

Hash Brown Potatoes

(Using dried hash browns)

1 & 3/4 cups dried hash brown potatoes
2 & 1/2 cups water
3 Tablespoons butter
Salt and pepper to taste

1). Bring the potatoes and water to a boil for 10 minutes. When most of the liquid is absorbed use half the butter and heat it up in a pan. When it is melted, spread the hash browns evenly in the pan and fry them until golden brown and tender.
2). Salt and pepper to taste. Lift the hash browns up with a spatula and melt the remaining butter. Flip the hash browns over. Fry until golden brown.
(Serves 4)

Hash Brown Potatoes

(Using fresh potatoes)

4-6 medium potatoes
2 quarts water
1/2 stick butter or 1/4 cup oil
Salt and pepper to taste

1). In a saucepan combine potatoes and water and bring them to a boil with their skins on. When the potatoes are cooked and a fork will penetrate into the potato easily, they are done. Cool them down by running cold water on them. Then peel and grate. It is best if you use the largest potato grater that you have.

2). Melt half the butter in a pan and place the hash brown potatoes on top of the butter. Fry until it is golden brown in color. Salt and pepper. Turn it over and fry on the other side. Salt and pepper.

(Serves 8)

Latkes (Potato Cakes)

2 pounds potatoes or 4 large russets
1/2 cup flour
1 teaspoon baking powder
2 eggs
1 small onion, finely chopped or grated
1 teaspoon salt
1/4 teaspoon pepper
vegetable or olive oil for frying

1). Peel the potatoes and grate them into a bowl of cold water to prevent them from browning.
2). Drain the water and pat the grated potatoes dry with a paper towel.
3). In a separate bowl beat together the flour, baking powder, eggs, and onion. Mix them with the potatoes and add the salt and pepper. Stir well.
4). In a heavy frying pan, heat up the oil. Drop about a table-spoon of potato mixture into the hot frying pan. Using a spatula, flatten the potato cake.
5). Fry it on one side until it is golden brown, then flip it over and cook the other side. Drain on a paper towel . Keep them warm in another pan or put them in the oven until all the latkes are fried. Continue making the potato cakes until the batter is used up. Serve warm with ketchup.
(Serves 4)

Old-Fashioned Fried Potatoes

8 slices bacon
6 large potatoes boiled and cooled
2 Tablespoons flour
Salt and pepper to taste
1/4 teaspoon seasoning salt
1/2 teaspoon paprika
1 teaspoon dried parsley
6 Tablespoons butter or bacon grease

1). Scrub and boil the potatoes in advance and let them cool. You can leave the skins on. The potatoes are done before they split and fall apart.
2). Fry the bacon until crisp. Set it aside, saving the grease.
3). Chop the potatoes into bite sized pieces or slices. Put the flour, seasoning salt, salt and pepper in a shaker bag and shake.
4). Melt the butter or bacon grease in a frying pan. Add the potatoes and fry until golden brown. Turn the potatoes until all sides are browned.
5). Top with crumbled bacon, dried parsley and paprika for color.

(Serves 6)

Roasted Garlic Sliced Potatoes

3 pounds or (6 medium sized potatoes)
1/2 cup melted butter
8 cloves garlic, crushed
3/4 cup grated parmesan cheese
1/2 teaspoon salt
1/2 teaspoon pepper

1). Peel and cut the potatoes into 1/4 inch slices. Rinse them and pat them dry on a paper towel and put them in a bowl.
2). In a small skillet, over medium heat, sauté the garlic in the butter for about 1 minute.
3). Add remaining ingredients (reserving half of the cheese mixture for later) and mix it with the potatoes.
4). Place the potato mixture in a greased (9x13) inch baking dish. Sprinkle the remaining cheese on top and bake at 400 degrees for 35 minutes until the top is golden brown.
(Serves 8)

Main and Side Dishes

Basic Potatoes Cooked in Milk

(This recipe is "Fabulous")

6 medium potatoes
4 Tablespoons flour
4-6 Tablespoons butter
Milk to cover potatoes
1/2 teaspoon onion salt
Salt and pepper to taste

1). Grate the potatoes with the largest grater that you have. Fill a (9x13) inch casserole dish with the potatoes.
2). Sprinkle the flour evenly on the top of the potatoes. Dot the top with small chunks of butter.
3). Barely cover the top of the potatoes with enough milk to moisten the potatoes. sprinkle the onion salt, salt, and pepper on top. Bake in a preheated oven at 375 degrees for 35-40 minutes.
(Serves 6)

Dorcas Anderson

Creamed Potatoes and Peas

10 small new red potatoes
1 can cream of chicken or celery soup
3/4 cup milk
1/2 teaspoon salt
Garlic powder to taste
1 cup frozen peas

1). Boil the potatoes with the skins on. Drain the water and add the peas. Set aside.
2). In a separate bowl, mix the creamed soup, milk, salt, and garlic powder together and blend well. Heat it to boiling. Pour the mixture over the top of the peas and potatoes.
(Serves 4-6)

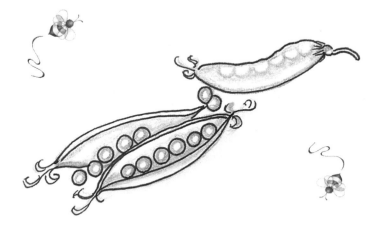

Crock Pot Onion Potatoes

6 medium potatoes diced
1/3 cup olive oil
1 package dry onion soup mix or 2 Tablespoons
dry mix
1/2 teaspoon salt
1/4 teaspoon pepper
3 minced cloves garlic
1/2 chopped onion
1 red or green pepper chopped

1). Combine the potatoes and oil in a bowl. Then add the remaining ingredients. Pour all ingredients into a slow cooker and cook on low for 6 hours or on high for 3 hours. These potatoes can also be cooked in the oven at 350-400 degrees for 45 minutes.
(Serves 6)

Mexican Tacos Over Potatoes

4-6 baked potatoes
1 pound ground beef
1 package taco seasoning mix
1 (16 oz.) can tomato sauce
1 (10 oz.) can of whole kernel corn

Toppings
1 cup shredded cheese
2 cups lettuce
2 chopped tomatoes
1/4 cup sour cream or ranch dressing

1). Fry the ground beef and drain the fat. Add the taco seasoning mix, tomato sauce, and corn.
2). Prepare the baked potatoes ahead by baking them in a 400 degree oven for 40-60 minutes. Cut a slit in the top and push the sides towards each other so the potato fluffs up in the middle. Put the taco mixture over the potato and top it with shredded cheese, lettuce, and tomatoes. Dab sour cream or ranch dressing on the top.
(Serves 4-6)

Potato and Ground Beef Hash

6 large potatoes
1 large onion, chopped
1 pound ground beef
1/2 teaspoon salt
1/8 teaspoon black pepper
1 Tablespoon butter for frying

1). In a saucepan covered with water boil the potatoes in their skins until cooked all the way through.
2). Let the potatoes cool down. Peel and cube them.
3). Fry the potatoes in the butter, add the onions and cook until the onions are transparent and potatoes are golden brown.
4). Fry the ground beef and mix all ingredients together. Serve warm.
(Serves 6)

Potato Quiche

6-8 cups cooked diced potatoes
1 & 1/2 cups grated cheddar cheese
4 Tablespoons finely chopped onion
2 Tablespoons butter
3 teaspoons salt
3 eggs
1/2 cup milk
1/4 teaspoon white pepper
1 & 1/2 cups additional grated cheddar cheese

1). Boil the potatoes, cool, peel, and dice them.
2). In a casserole dish layer the potatoes and cheese, sprinkling each layer with onion. Break the butter up into small pats and place on top of the potato mixture.
3). Mix the eggs, milk, and seasonings together and pour over the potato mixture.
4). Sprinkle the additional cheese on top of the casserole.
5). Bake at
325 degrees
for 45 minutes.
(Serves 12)

65

Shepherds' Pie

(This recipe is "Fabulous")

1 pound ground beef
2 onions chopped
1 cup diced carrots
1-2 cloves garlic, minced
1 Tablespoon flour
1 cup beef bouillon
7 ounces canned, chopped, tomatoes
1 teaspoon Worcestershire sauce
1 teaspoon chopped fresh sage or (1/2 teaspoon dried sage)
1 & 3/4 cup mushrooms, (optional)
6 medium potatoes
2 Tablespoons butter
3-4 Tablespoons milk
Salt and pepper to taste

1). Pre boil the potatoes in enough water to cover them. Add a pinch of salt. While the potatoes are boiling, brown the ground beef until cooked and browned. Crumble the meat, add onions, carrots, and garlic, and continue to cook for about 10 minutes.

2). Stir in the flour and continue cooking for a couple of minutes. Gradually add the beef bouillon, bringing it to a full boil.

3). Add the chopped tomatoes, Worcestershire sauce, herbs and seasonings. Cover and Simmer on low heat for 25 minutes. Stir in the mushrooms and line the bottom of a casserole dish with the meat mixture.

4). When the potatoes are tender, drain the water off them and mash them with butter, milk, salt and pepper. Put the mashed potatoes in a large pastry bag with a large star tip. Use the pastry bag to decorate the top of the meat mixture, by squeezing out the potatoes in a decorative manner with long strips side by side, covering the entire meat mixture.

5). Preheat the oven to 400 degrees. Cook the Shepherds Pie until it is heated all the way through and the potatoes are golden brown. Serve it hot. (Serves 6-8)

Stroganoff Over Potatoes

2 beef steaks cut into strips
1/2 cup chopped onion
1 Tablespoon butter
1 (10 oz.) can cream of mushroom soup
1/2 cup sliced mushrooms
1/2 cup sour cream
2 Tablespoons ketchup
1 teaspoon Worcestershire sauce
1 teaspoon minced garlic
1/4 teaspoon paprika
1/4 teaspoon salt
1/8 teaspoon pepper
4 cups mashed potatoes or 4 baked potatoes

1). Fry the beef strips and onion in the butter. Stir until slightly browned.
2). Stir in the remaining ingredients except the potatoes. Simmer another 10 minutes.
3). Place the stroganoff over the potatoes. Either baked or mashed.
(Serves 4)

Tater Tot Casserole

2 pounds hamburger
2 small cans of cream of mushroom soup
1 soup can of milk
2 Tablespoons dried onion or 1/4 cup chopped onion
1/2 cup sour cream
1 bag of tator tots
1 & 1/2 cups shredded cheddar cheese
4 cups of crushed corn flakes

1). Grease a large casserole dish and layer a (11x13) casserole dish with tater tots.
2). Mix all the other ingredients together except the cheese and cornflakes.
3). Pour the mixture over the tator tots and sprinkle with the cheese.
4). Top it with crushed corn flakes.
5). Bake at 350 degrees for 45 minutes until hot and bubbly.
(Serves 8)

Mashed Potatoes

Cottage Cheese Potato Casserole

(This recipe is "Fabulous")

4 large potatoes peeled, cubed, and boiled
6 ounces of cottage cheese
4 ounces of sour cream
Salt and pepper to taste
2 scallion onions chopped
1/2 stick of butter
Paprika

1). Precook the potatoes by boiling in enough water to cover them. Drain the water off the potatoes. Put all ingredients except butter and onions in a bowl.
2). Beat well with a mixer or a potato masher. Add scallion onions and mix well.
3). Put potato mixture in a (9x13) inch greased casserole dish.
4). Cut the butter up into chunks and place on top of the potato mixture.
5). Sprinkle with paprika for color
6). Bake at 350 degrees for 30 minutes.
(Serves 8)

Cream Cheese Mashed Potato Casserole

4 large potatoes cooked and mashed to
equal 4 cups mashed potatoes
Milk and butter to moisten
1 (8-oz) package cream cheese
1/2 onion chopped
2 eggs
2 Tablespoons flour
Salt and pepper to taste
1 can french fried onions

1). Pre cook the potatoes. Drain the water. Mash the potatoes
with a little milk and butter to moisten or use instant potatoes
reconstituted.
2). Add the cream cheese, chopped onion, egg, flour, salt, and
pepper.
3). Put the potato mixture in a (9x13) casserole baking dish
and top with french onions. (French fried onions can be found
in a can usually in the section of the grocery store with the
breadcrumbs or other toppings).
4). Bake at 300 degrees for 35 minutes.
(Serves 6)

Creamy Mashed Potatoes

(Using dried potato flakes or pearls)

3 & 1/2 cups hot water
1/3 cup powdered milk
1 Tablespoon butter or butter powder
1/4 teaspoon salt to taste
2 cups potato flakes, granules, or pearls

1). In a medium sauce pan, combine all ingredients together except dried potatoes. Bring to a boil, then add the potatoes.
2). Stir over medium heat until the potatoes fluff up and thicken. Let the potatoes set until all the water is absorbed. (Serves 6)

Fluffy Mashed Potatoes

8 medium potatoes peeled
1/2 teaspoon salt for water
2 Tablespoons butter
1/4-1/2 cup hot milk or half and half
Salt and pepper to taste

1). Peel the potatoes and cut them in quarters.
2). In a large saucepan, boil the potatoes in enough water to cover them. Add 1/2 teaspoon of salt to the water. Boil for 15 to 20 minutes or until the potatoes are very soft. Drain water.
3). Mash the potatoes, and slowly add the butter and milk. Add the milk slowly until the potatoes are nice and fluffy. You may not use all the milk, add enough to make it a good consistency. Salt and pepper to taste.
(Serves 8)

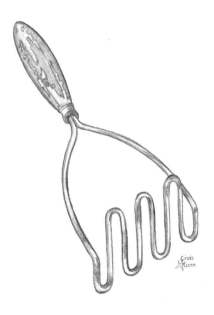

Roasted Garlic Mashed Potatoes

   To make roasted garlic mashed potatoes, Use the previous recipe for mashed potatoes and add this variation. Roast 6-8 unpeeled garlic cloves in a tin foil envelope with a little olive oil, salt, and pepper sprinkled on top. Roast for 40 minutes at 400 degrees F. Peel the garlic and add peeled, roasted, and mashed garlic cloves to the mashed potatoes and blend well. Sprinkle with paprika for color.
(Serves 4)

Mashed Potato Balls

2 cups mashed potatoes
1/4 cup chopped ham or bacon, cooked and
crumbled
1 Tablespoon chopped parsley
Salt and pepper to taste
2 eggs well beaten
1 cup bread crumbs
Vegetable oil for frying

1). If you are using fresh potatoes, peel and cube 4 medium sized potatoes and place them in a sauce pan. Cover with water and boil until tender. Drain the water and mash the potatoes. Add a little butter and 1 tablespoon of milk to make them light and fluffy. (If you are using dried potato flakes or pearls combine 1 cup potato flakes with 2 cups boiling water. Mix well until it is light and fluffy). To the 2 cups of mashed potatoes, add ham or bacon, parsley, salt and pepper. Mix well.

2). Drop by spoonfuls in a hot frying pan with a little oil. Cook on all sides for one minute, take the balls out of the oil.

3). Dip the balls into the beaten eggs and roll them in bread crumbs.

4). Cook them again in the hot oil and turn them several times until they are golden brown on all sides. Eat them as a side dish.

(Serves 4)

Oven Baked Mashed Potatoes and Cheese

(Using fresh or dried potato pearls)

3 cups mashed potatoes or (1 & 1/2 cups potato pearls or flakes mixed with 3 cups boiling water)
1/4 cup dried onions
3 & 1/2 Tablespoons dried cheese powder
2 Tablespoons water
1/4 teaspoon paprika
1/2 teaspoon salt
1/4 teaspoon pepper
1/4 teaspoon garlic powder
paprika for color

1). Soak the onions in enough water to cover them for about 10 minutes. Drain off all excess liquid. Add the onions, spices, and 1/2 tablespoon cheese powder together. Mix well and spread in the bottom of a small casserole dish. spread the potatoes over the cheese mixture. Mix the remaining cheese powder with 2 tablespoons water, and drizzle over the top of the potatoes. Sprinkle with paprika. Bake at 350 degrees for 15 minutes. (Serves 4)

Salads

German Potato Salad

6 medium potatoes
1 (12 oz) package of bacon
4 scallion green onions
1 cup sugar
1 cup hot water
3/4 cup cider vinegar
3 Tablespoons corn starch

1). Boil the potatoes with the skins on until they are cooked all the way through.
2). Drain the water off the potatoes and let them cool down until they can be peeled and sliced. Slice to 1/4 inch thick.
3). Cut the bacon into small pieces and fry it until it is crisp. Pat the bacon with a paper towel. Save 1/2 cup bacon to sprinkle on top of the salad.
4). Slice up the green onions and fry them in the bacon grease. Save 1/3 cup of grease.
5). Add the water, sugar, and vinegar to the fried onion and bacon grease. Boil it on low heat until the sugar is melted.
6). Dissolve the corn starch in a small amount of the liquid to keep it from getting lumpy. Add the mixture to the water, sugar, and vinegar. Add remaining corn starch. Continue cooking until the mixture is clear and thickened.
7). Toss potatoes and all ingredients together until mixed. Top with crumbled bacon pieces.
(Serves 12-15)

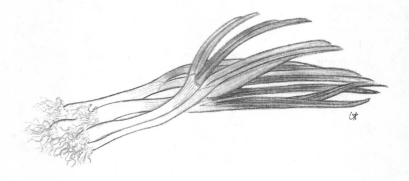

Hawaiian Macaroni and Potato Salad

(This recipe is "Fabulous")

6-8 large potatoes
4-8 hard boiled eggs
4 cups precooked macaroni
4 cups mayonnaise
3 teaspoons mustard (to taste)
3 teaspoons pickle relish
1 teaspoon salt
1/2 teaspoon pepper
1/2 lb. imitation crab meat

1). Wash, and boil the potatoes in enough water to cover them. When the potatoes are cooked all the way through but still firm, drain off the boiling water and run the potatoes under cold water to cool them down. When they are cool enough to handle, cube them into bite sized pieces.
2). Boil the eggs, and cool them down. Cut into bite sized pieces.
3). Precook the macaroni and drain the water.
4). In a large bowl, mix all remaining ingredients together except crab. Add the mayonnaise sauce to the other ingredients. Mix well. Add crab and mix well.
5). This dish is famous at Hawaiian Luau's. It feeds a crowd. You will be amazed at the delicious flavor. It is better if it sits in the refrigerator over night to chill and marinate. (Serves 12-15)

Jan TiaTia

79

Hot Potato Salad

8 medium sized potatoes
1 (12 ounce) package of bacon
1 medium sized red onion
1 green pepper
3 hard boiled eggs
2/3 cup vinegar
1 Tablespoon sugar
1 teaspoon salt
2 Tablespoons water

1). Boil the potatoes until cooked all the way through. When cool, peel and dice them.
2). Cut the bacon into small pieces and fry them until crisp. Remove the bacon from the grease and mix the onion, pepper and eggs together.
3). In a separate bowl add the vinegar, sugar, salt, and water.
4). Mix all the ingredients together and heat the potato salad in a saucepan. Keep it on a low temperature. Do not over mix it or it will go mushy.
5). Serve it hot.
(Serves 8)

Marinated Potato Salad

4 cups cooked, diced, cold potatoes
2 scallion onions, chopped
1 & 1/2 teaspoons salt
1/2 teaspoon paprika
French dressing (enough to moisten)
3 hard-boiled eggs
1 Tablespoon dried parsley
Mayonnaise to moisten

1). Mix the potatoes, onion, salt, and paprika together in a
bowl. Add the French dressing, just enough to moisten the
potatoes and marinate for about 1 hour in the refrigerator.
2). Just before serving, add sliced boiled eggs, parsley, and
enough mayonnaise to moisten.
3). Serve on crisp lettuce leaves and garnish with tomato
wedges. This recipe has an orange color which is odd, but it is
very delicious.
(Serves 8-10)

New York Style Deli Potato Salad

5 pounds new red potatoes
1/2 cup grated carrots
1/4 cup red bell pepper
1/4 cup green bell pepper
1/4 cup chopped fresh parsley

Dressing
1 & 1/2 cups real mayonnaise
1/4 cup white vinegar or pickle juice
1 Tablespoon salt
1/2 Tablespoon ground pepper
1/2 Tablespoon dry mustard

1). Prepare the potatoes by boiling them in enough water to cover them. Do not overcook. Cut them into 1/8 inch thick round slices. Grate the carrots and chop the bell peppers and parsley. Mix this all together. Set aside.
2). Prepare the dressing by mixing all the ingredients together. Add the potato vegetable mixture. Mix well . If the dressing is a little thick, thin it with some buttermilk or milk.
3). Refrigerate for 24 hours. The salad tastes the best after it has marinated in the dressing. sprinkle paprika on top for color.
(Serves 12)

Russian Potato Salad

4 large potatoes
1/2 small onion grated
1/2 teaspoon celery seed
1 teaspoon salt
2 teaspoons sugar
1/4 teaspoon pepper
1/2 cup Russian dressing
1/2 cup mayonnaise
1 Tablespoon vinegar
10 radishes sliced
1 & 1/2 cups chopped celery

1). Boil potatoes in their skins. Pour off the water and cool the potatoes enough to handle them. Cut them into cubes.
2). Add the seasonings first, then the dressing, mayonnaise, and vinegar.
3). Before serving add the sliced radishes and celery. Toss it all together and moisten with more Russian dressing if needed. (Russian dressing can be purchased from the grocery store). (Serves 6)

Traditional Potato Salad

(This recipe is "Fabulous")

3 pounds or (12-14) medium sized potatoes
1 large green pepper diced
1 large carrot, peeled and grated
2 dill pickles diced
2 green scallion onions, chopped
2/3 cup mayonnaise
2 Tablespoons lemon juice
1 teaspoon salt
1/2 teaspoon garlic powder
1/4 teaspoon pepper
1/2 teaspoon dry mustard

1). In a cooking pot, boil the potatoes until they are tender.
Drain and cool. Peel the skins off the potatoes and cut them
up into cubes.
2). Combine the cubed potatoes, green peppers, carrot,
pickle, and green onions in a large bowl. Mix well and set aside.
3). Mix remaining ingredients together to make the mayonnaise
mixture. Pour it over the potatoes and stir well. Chill in the
refrigerator. (Serves 12-15)

Soups, Chowders, and Stews

Creamed Corn Soup

(This recipe is "Fabulous")

4 large potatoes, peeled and cubed
1 large onion, peeled and cubed
1 (14.5 oz) can whole kernel corn
1 (14.5 oz) can creamed corn
3 teaspoons or cubes of chicken bouillon
2 (10 oz.) cans cream of chicken soup
6-10 ounces cooked ham

1). Put the potatoes and onion in a large pot. Drain the corn juice into the pot. Add 3 cups water and the bullion cubes. Bring to a boil for 10 minutes or until tender.
2). Add cans of corn and cream of chicken soup. Add the Ham and heat until warm .
3). Add the cream cheese. Heat and stir until blended. Do not boil.
(Serves 6)

Carol Wayman

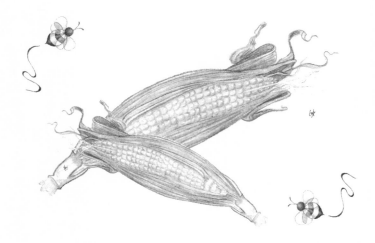

86

Cream of Potato Soup

8 slices bacon
4 teaspoons chopped onion
2 teaspoons dried parsley
4 teaspoons chopped celery
2 diced carrots
1 teaspoon salt
1/4 teaspoon white pepper
6 medium Idaho potatoes (save the potato water)
2 Tablespoons butter
2 Tablespoons flour
2 quarts boiling potato water
2 cups powdered dry milk

1). Cook and crumble bacon. Add the onion, parsley, celery, carrots, salt, and pepper to the bacon grease. Simmer for ten minutes. Stir often

2). Peel potatoes and dice into bite sized pieces. Add the potatoes and vegetables, simmer for 2 minutes. Add water and boil for 20 minutes until tender.

3). In a separate skillet melt the 2 tablespoons butter and add the flour, stirring to prevent lumps. Slowly add a cup of the potato liquid and stir until it thickens. Add the dry milk to the water and vegetables. Stir until it dissolves. Add this to the soup.

4). For variation, add other cooked vegetables.

(Serves 6)

87

Manhattan Tomato Clam Chowder

3 large potatoes
1/2 pound bacon
1 large onion (chopped)
2 carrots sliced thin
2 large stalks celery sliced thin
1 Tablespoon chopped fresh parsley
1 (28 oz) can stewed tomatoes
1 & 1/2 teaspoons salt
1/4 teaspoon pepper
3 (6 oz) cans of clams with the liquid
1 bay leaf
1 teaspoon thyme (dried and crushed)

1). Peel the potatoes and cut them up into dices.
2). Fry the bacon and cut into pieces.
3). Prepare all the vegetables.
4). Mix all ingredients together and cook on the stove until the vegetables are tender or put all ingredients in a crock pot and cook for 8 hours on low, or until the vegetables are tender.
(Serves 6)

New England Clam or Seafood Chowder

(This recipe is "Fabulous")

3 slices of bacon cut into pieces
1 cup diced and peeled potatoes
1/2 cup chopped celery
1/4 cup chopped onion
1/4 teaspoon salt
1/8 teaspoon dried thyme
1/8 teaspoon pepper
2 (6 ounce) cans minced clams, reserve liquid
or 2 pounds fresh or frozen fish such as cod,
haddock, salmon etc..
1/4 cup all purpose flour
3 cups milk

1). Fry the bacon and crumble.
2). Add the potatoes, celery, onions, salt, thyme, and pepper
to the bacon grease and fry until tender. Add clam juice, bring
to a boil. Reduce heat to low, cover and simmer for 5 minutes.
3). In a small bowl, combine flour and milk, stirring until lumps
are gone. Gradually stir the flour and milk mixture into the
vegetables. Cook over medium heat. stir constantly until the
mixture thickens. Add the clams (with liquid) or fish, stir well,
and continue cooking.
4). Place bacon bits on top of soup.
(Serves 4)

Potato Broccoli Soup

4 large potatoes, peeled and cubed
1 large onion, peeled and cubed
3 cubes or 3 teaspoons chicken bouillon
2 crowns of broccoli chopped or 1 (16 oz) package of chopped broccoli
2 (10 oz) cans cream of chicken soup
1 cup chicken cubed or (6-10 ounces) canned chicken with broth.
1 (8 oz) package of cream cheese

1). Place onion and potatoes in a large pot. cover with 1 quart of water. Add the chicken bullion. Boil for 10 minutes or until tender.
2). Add the chopped broccoli to the potatoes and boil for 2 minutes.
3). Add the canned soup and stir well. Add the chicken. Heat all the way through.
4). Turn off the heat and add the cream cheese. Stir until blended. Do not boil.
(Serves 8)

Carol Wayman

Potato Corn Chowder

(This recipe is "Fabulous")

1 (12 ounce) package bacon fried and crumbled
2 (15-ounce) cans whole kernel corn
1 cup chopped onion
1 cup peeled and cubed potatoes
1 cup water
4 teaspoons or cubes of chicken bouillon
2 Tablespoons butter
2 & 1/2 Tablespoons flour
2 cups milk
1/2 cup shredded cheddar cheese

1). Fry bacon and crumble. Combine the first six ingredients together. Bring this mixture to a boil and reduce heat. Cover and simmer for (7- 10) minutes or until potatoes are tender, stir often.
2). Melt the butter in a saucepan, and add the flour to the butter. Stirring to avoid lumps. Add the milk a little at a time, beating until the mixture is thick.
3). Add the flour, butter and milk mixture to the vegetable mixture. Cook and stir until the soup is thick and bubbly.
4). Sprinkle cheese on top.
(Serves 8)

Potato Dumpling Soup

(This recipe is 'Fabulous")

1/2 pound of cooked ground beef
1/2 cup each of carrots, celery, potatoes, and onions
Salt and pepper to taste
6 cups beef broth

Dumplings
2/3 cup mashed potatoes
1 & 1/4 cups flour
4 teaspoons baking powder
1 teaspoon salt
2 teaspoons butter
1/2 cup milk

1). To make the soup, first fry the ground beef, and drain the grease. Fry the vegetables in a little butter until tender, add them together with the, salt, pepper, and broth.
2). In a separate bowl mix all remaining ingredients together into a dough. On a floured surface roll out the dough in a long rope about 1 inch thick. Cut 1 inch pieces off the rope and roll them into balls. Cook the balls by drop-
ping them into the
pot of vegetable
beef soup.
(Serves 8)

Potato Dumplings for Stew

2 cups mashed potatoes
1 egg
1/4 cup flour
1 Tablespoon minced onion
1 Tablespoon chopped parsley
1/2 teaspoon salt

1). In a bowl, whip the eggs together and combine all other ingredients, mixing well.
2). Drop by rounded tablespoons in a pot of hot stew. Make sure the stew is fully cooked. Cover and simmer for 20 minutes. The Dumplings will puff up and float to the top of the stew when they are cooked.
(Serves 12)

Red Potato Stew

6 red potatoes cut in cubes
4 carrots
1/2 large onion
2 stalks celery
1/2 green pepper
3 teaspoons or 3 cubes beef bouillon
3 cups water
Salt and pepper to taste
1/2 lb cooked ground beef

1). Wash and cut up potatoes with skins
2). Cut the carrots into slices about (1 inch) thick.
3). Chop up the onion, celery, and green pepper.
4). In a stew pot mix the vegetables and the bouillon, water, salt, and pepper together.
5). Precook the hamburger and drain the grease. Add the meat to the stew.
6). Cook until the vegetables are tender, about a half hour on the stove or several hours in the crock pot.
7). If dumplings are desired, use the former recipe for dumplings, and add them to the stew. This makes a very hearty stew.
(Serves 8)

Sour Cream Baked Potato Soup

4 large potatoes
6 slices bacon
6 cups milk
1/2 cup white flour
6 green scallion onions sliced
1 & 1/2 cups cheddar cheese grated
3/4 teaspoon salt
1/4 teaspoon pepper
1 cup sour cream

1). Pierce potatoes and wrap them in tin foil. Bake them in a 350 degree oven for 40-50 minutes.
2). In a large skillet, fry and crumble the bacon. Place the bacon in a small bowl to be used later.
3). In another small bowl mix the milk and flour together. Using the same skillet that the bacon was fried in, add the milk and flour mixture to the bacon grease. Using a wire wisk, beat the mixture, stir constantly and cook over medium heat until it is thick and bubbly.
4). Cut the baked potatoes in half and scoop out the potato. Mash the potatoes in a bowl with a little milk and butter. Add the potatoes, half of the bacon, chopped onions, grated cheese, salt, and pepper to the milk mixture. Add sour cream and cook one minute longer.
5). Place soup in bowls and top with onion, bacon and cheese. (Serves 6)

Sweet Potatoes

Candied Sweet Potatoes

4 large sweet potatoes
1/2 cup or 1 square butter
1/4 cup boiling water
1/2 cup brown sugar
1/2 cup shredded coconut (optional)

1). Wash the sweet potatoes and place them in a saucepan with enough water to cover them. Boil them until they are tender. Drain the water off and run cold water over them to cool them down.
2). When they are cool, peel the sweet potatoes and cut them into 1/4 inch slices. Layer them in a (9x13) inch casserole dish.
3). Mix remaining ingredients except coconut together and pour the syrup over the sweet potatoes.
4). Bake them in the oven at 350 degrees for 1 hour or until the potatoes are tender. Sprinkle with coconut and continue baking for a few minutes longer until the coconut is slightly brown on top.
(Serves 4)

Cranberry Sweet Potatoes

2 (1-lb 12 oz) cans of cooked sweet potatoes
3/4 cup canned cranberry sauce
2 Tablespoons water
2 Tablespoons brown sugar
1/4 cup melted butter
1/4 teaspoon salt

1). Slice the sweet potatoes into 1/4 inch thick slices. Layer 1/2 the potatoes in the bottom of a 2 quart casserole dish.
2). Combine remaining ingredients together and pour half the mixture over the sweet potatoes.
3). Layer the remaining sweet potatoes over the mixture and top it off with the remaining cranberry sauce mixture.
4). Add chopped walnuts to the top of the casserole and bake for 45 minutes in a 350 degree oven. The flavor of this traditional sweet potato recipe is surprisingly delicious.
(Serves 8)

Creamy Sweet Potato and Leek Soup

2 cups leeks (2 large)
2 Tablespoons extra-virgin olive oil
4 cloves minced fresh garlic
3 cups peeled and cooked sweet potatoes (4 large)
32 oz. can of chicken or vegetable broth
8 oz. (or more) water
Salt and pepper to taste
1 tsp. hot pepper sauce

1). Clean the leeks thoroughly, remove the tough outer layer off the leeks, slice lengthwise and again widthwise.
2). In a heavy frying pan add the olive oil and leeks. Cook on high for a minute, then reduce heat to medium low. Sauté briefly until translucent (3-4 minutes), stirring often. Remove and reserve half a cup of leeks.
3). Add the minced garlic and stir one more minute. Add the cooked sweet potato, and broth, stir to mix well. Add water to achieve desired consistency.
4). Increase heat and bring soup to a simmer, seasoning with salt, pepper, and hot sauce to taste. In a blender, purée or use a handheld blender directly into the pot. Put the reserved leeks back into soup.
5). This soup can be made ahead, refrig-erated, and reheat-ed. Make sure to serve it hot.
(Serves 8)

Note: To thin the soup add more chick-en broth. This recipe makes a wonderful "sauce" over chicken, fish, or pasta.

Sweet Potato, Lemon and Banana Salad

3 cups sweet potatoes (diced)
4 Tablespoons butter
1 Tablespoon lemon juice
2 cloves garlic (minced)
1 red bell pepper (chopped)
1 green bell pepper (chopped)
2 firm or green bananas
2 Tablespoons butter
4 slices white bread
Salt and pepper to taste

Dressing
2 Tablespoons olive oil
2 Tablespoons lemon juice
2 Tablespoons chives (chopped)
2 Tablespoons honey

1). Wash, peel, and dice the sweet potatoes. Cook in a pan of boiling water for 10-15 minutes or until tender. Drain the water off the potatoes and set aside for later.
2). Melt the butter in a skillet. Add the lemon juice, minced garlic, and chopped bell peppers. Stirring constantly for about 3 minutes longer.
3). Slice the bananas into 1 inch pieces. Add the bananas to the skillet and continue cooking for 1 more minute. Remove the bananas from the pan and put them in with the sweet potatoes,
4). In a separate skillet, melt 2 tablespoons butter and fry the cut up, cubed bread. Stir until both sides of bread are golden brown. Set the croutons aside to put on top of the salad.
5). In a small bowl combine the oil, lemon juice, chopped chives, and honey together to make a sauce for the salad.
6). In a salad bowl, combine all ingredients except dressing and croutons. Salt and pepper to taste. Pour dressing over the salad and top with the croutons.
(Serves 4)

Sweet Potato Cashew Casserole

4 sweet potatoes cut lengthwise in half
Boiling water with a little salt
1 teaspoon ground cinnamon
1/4 teaspoon salt
1 egg
1/4 cup pineapple or orange juice
1/4 cup sugar
3 Tablespoons melted butter
1/2 cup salted cashews (chopped)

1). In a saucepan cook the sweet potatoes in enough water to cover. Boil until they are tender, (about 30 minutes). Drain the water. When they are cool enough to touch, peel the sweet potatoes and mash them until they are fluffy.
2). Add cinnamon, salt, egg, juice, and sugar. Beat until fluffy. If the mixture seems dry, add more juice. Mix in 2 table-spoons of the melted butter.
3). Spoon the batter into a small casserole dish.
4). In a small frying pan, melt the butter and add the cashews. Stir them until they are lightly toasted on both sides. Sprinkle on top of the casserole.
5). Bake in a preheated oven at 375 degrees for 20 minutes until completely cooked.
(Serves 4)

Sweet Potato Casserole

3 cups cooked, mashed sweet potatoes
1 cup sugar
1 teaspoon vanilla
1/2 cup melted butter
1/2 cup milk
2 eggs (beaten)

Topping
1/2 cup brown sugar
1/4 cup flour
2 & 1/2 Tablespoons melted butter
1/2 cups chopped pecans

1). Mix first 6 ingredients together. Pour into a (9x13) inch casserole dish, flatten out the sweet potatoes.
2). In another bowl, mix all topping ingredients and sprinkle over the top of the sweet potato mixture.
3). Bake in a preheated oven at 350 degrees for 45 minutes, or until the casserole is golden brown and bubbly on top.
(Serves 6)

Sweet Potato Custard

(This recipe is "Fabulous")

4 cups raw, cubed or 2 cups canned sweet
potatoes
1 Tablespoon melted butter
3/4 cup brown sugar
3 eggs
3 Tablespoons milk
1 Tablespoon lemon juice
1 lemon rind grated
1 cup dried apple slices (chopped)
2 teaspoons baking powder
1 cup whipped cream for topping

1). Boil the sweet potatoes in enough water to cover them.
When they are soft, drain the water and mash them until
smooth.
2). Mix together the hot sweet potatoes, butter and sugar.
Beat in the remaining ingredients, mixing well.
3). Grease a square (8 inch) cake pan. Pour the mixture into
the pan.
4). Preheat the oven to 325 degrees. Place the pan in the oven
and bake 1 hour or more. The custard is done if a toothpick
inserted into the middle comes out clean.
5). Take the custard out of the pan and cool on a wire rack.
Top with whipped cream.
(Serves 6)

103

Sweet Potatoes Glazed with Orange

6-8 medium sweet potatoes or 1 large can of canned sweet potatoes or yams
(optional) alternate sliced apples and sweet potatoes (4 sweet potatoes and 4 apples)
1 teaspoon salt
2 Tablespoons butter
3 Tablespoons orange juice with grated rind
1/4 teaspoon salt
3/4 cup dark corn syrup

1). Wash the sweet potatoes and place them in a saucepan covered with water. Add the 1 teaspoon of salt.
2). Boil the potatoes for 30 minutes or until barely tender. Peel the potatoes and slice them about 3/4 inch thick. Place them in a casserole dish. If using apples, cook them first then layer them with the sweet potatoes.
3). In a saucepan, combine remaining ingredients. Bring to a boil and pour over the sweet potatoes.
Bake at 350 degrees for 30 minutes.
(Serves 8-10)

notes...

notes...

Books and other products available from Peggy Layton

Dried Potato Products

Dried Potato Products available. Call or e-mail for current prices and shipping charges.

We sell dried potato slices, dices, hash brown potatoes, Potato flakes, granules, and pearls. We also sell dried cheese, milk, and butter. These are all sold in gallon size #10 cans, sealed with nitrogen and packaged for long term storage.

Books Available

Cookin' With Home Storage
  $15.95
Cookin' With Beans And Rice
  $12.95

Cookin' With Powdered Milk
  $9.50
Cookin' With Dried Eggs
  $7.50
"Food Storage 101" Where do I begin?
  $12.95
Emergency Food Storage And Survival Handbook
  $15.95
Cookin' With Kids In The Kitchen
  $12.95
Funeral Potatoes & Other Potato Recipes to Die for
  $12.95
Shipping and handling $3.50 for the first book and an additional $.75 cents for each additional book.

Wholesale prices as well as Church
or Civic Group discounts available
for quantity sales.

Check out our web page at
www.PeggyLayton.net

Questions, e-mail me at
splayton@sisna.com

Mail in orders
to
Peggy Layton
P.O. Box 44
Manti, Utah
84642

Phone orders 435-835-0311
Cell Phone 435-851-0777

We accept Visa, Mastercard,
and Discover on
internet and phone orders.